Struggle To Be Borne

By the same artists:

Home Street Home, 1984

Struggle To Be Borne

Kira Corser
Photography

Fran Adler
Poetry

Foreword by W. Benson Harer, Jr., M.D.

SAN DIEGO STATE UNIVERSITY PRESS
San Diego, Ca.
1988

Struggle To Be Borne
Companion volume to the traveling exhibit.

First printing, January, 1988.

Cover and book design by Ron Coviello

Library of Congress
ISBN   0-916304-84-1

For our children,
for the children

Contents

Foreword

On behalf of the American College of Obstetricians and Gynecologists, I would like to express my deep gratitude to Kira and Fran for their work in the exhibit "Struggle To Be Borne." For through their eyes, ears and hearts, they are helping to open the eyes of the world to the problems faced by pregnant, poor women in San Diego, California and the nation. It is our hope that by utilizing art, where politics have failed, that someday soon, access to prenatal care will no longer be a privilege of the few, but a right of all women.

Dr. Key expressed it best in the exhibit when he said,

"When a woman is denied care we are regressing to the 1900's, to the turn of the century, with no prenatal care."

It is incredible that in 1987 and in the wealthiest nation in the world, the number of women who receive late or no prenatal care continues to increase. And we know that babies born to women who receive no prenatal care are three times more likely to die in infancy. How many babies will continue to be born too small, too soon, before we as individuals, as a nation, say, "Enough."

Kira and Fran, thank you for opening our eyes and hearts to the problems faced by poor, pregnant women, fathers and children.

W. Benson Harer, Jr., M.D.
Chairman
California (District IX)
American College of
Obstetricians and Gynecologists

Acknowledgments

We would like to thank the National Endowment for the Arts, the City of San Diego, and the Combined Arts and Education Council (COMBO), as well as Dave Copley and the March of Dimes, for their support which enabled us to complete the *Struggle To Be Borne* exhibit and book.

Special thanks go to Dr. Marilyn J. Boxer, Dean of the College of Arts and Letters, San Diego State University, and her associates at the SDSU Press, for ensuring the timely availability of the book at the exhibit opening in the State Capitol Building, Sacramento, California, January 1988.

Our appreciation is also extended to KPBS Television and KPBS Radio Station for their support and encouragement.

Grateful acknowledgment is made to Adrienne Rich, for her permission to use a line (page 42) from her poem "An Old House in America," *The Fact of a Door Frame* (W.W. Norton & Co.), page 222.

The poems, "Underground," and "Mother Tongue," first appeared in *Pacific Review*, Summer, 1986, and Winter, 1986.

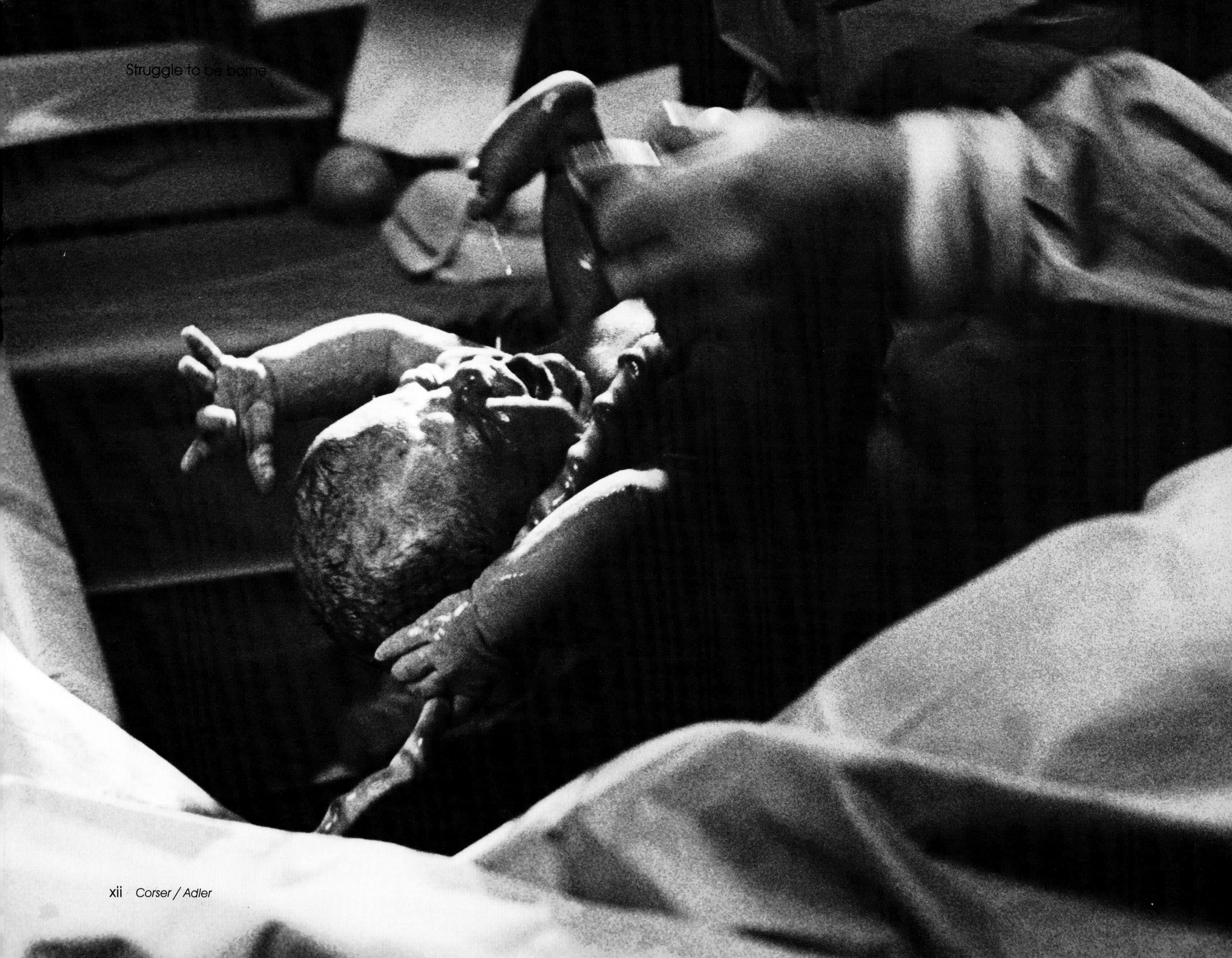
Struggle to be borne

Preface

One in five of the babies birthed in San Diego in 1987 will be borne by and born to a woman struggling to find care.

In 1987, a time when costly technology and test-tubes have cracked open both outer and inner space, one in five pregnant women will go without care as basic as vitamins and checkups.

In San Diego, as across the country, due to rising malpractice and low Medi-Cal insurance rates, fewer and fewer obstetricians are delivering babies of poor women. In 1985, of the more than 220 San Diego obstetricians, only ninety-seven would deliver women covered by Medi-Cal insurance. In 1987, those doctors have dwindled to eleven.

Because of this, more and more women have turned to prenatal programs at community clinics, staffed by nurse midwives. Even there, they are being turned away. In 1985, the clinics could serve only 100 women each month, turning away 200 more. And the crisis is increasing. In January 1987 alone, the clinics had to turn away 643 women, an increase of 300 percent.

What do these women — about 7,000 to 8,000 of them — do? Many arrive in hospital emergency rooms in labor. Some are turned away, sent by taxi to another hospital. Their babies — without prenatal care — are born too small and too early, and spend weeks, even months, hooked up to costly machines, struggling to survive.

This photography-poetry exhibit attempts to penetrate the denial surrounding the crisis of thousands of San Diego women — and hundreds of thousands of women across the country — who are pregnant, poor, and shut out from care.

Kira Corser
Fran Adler

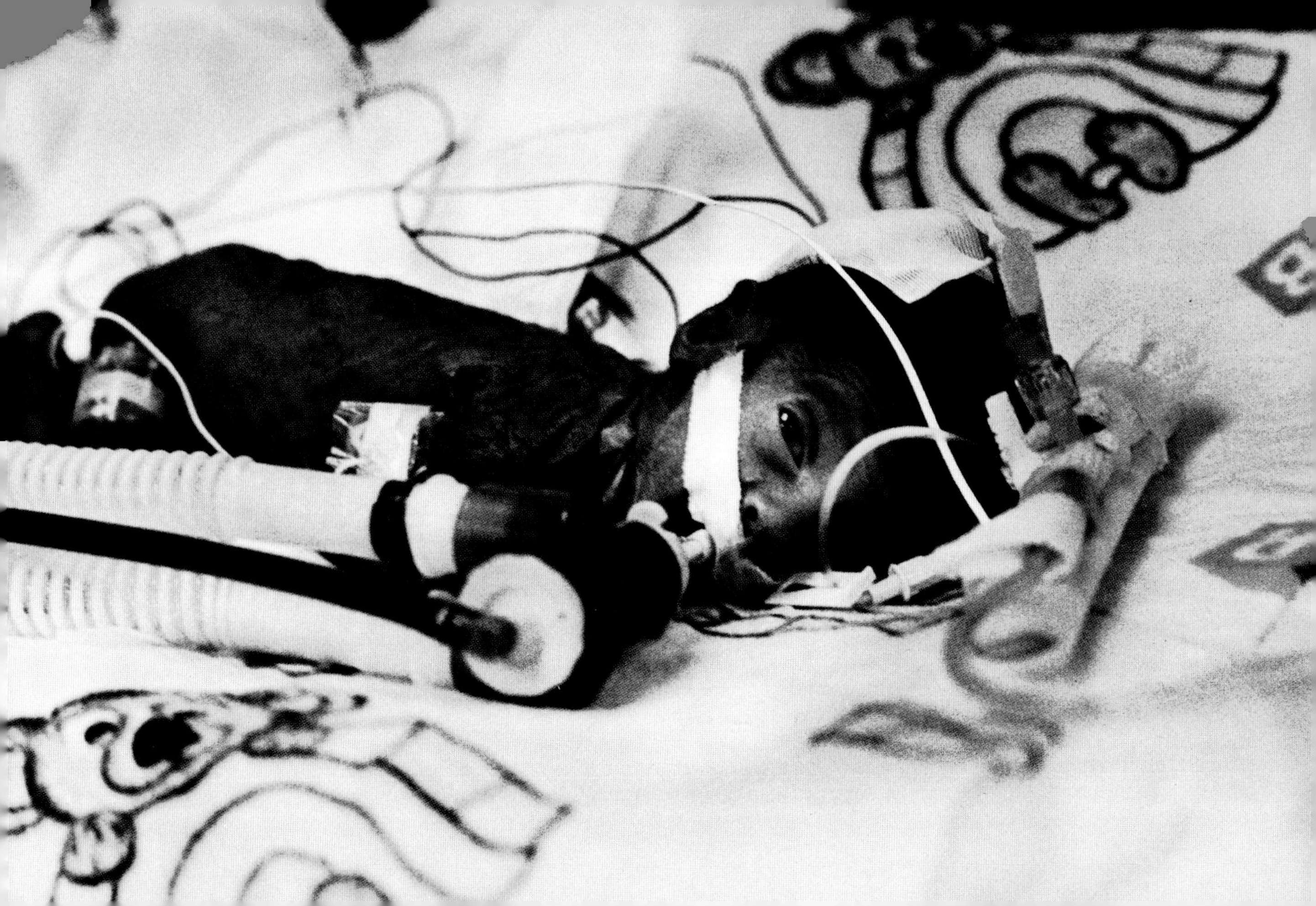

Joshua

I could hold you, Joshua,
in the palm of my life,
cup my forty years
around your hanging flesh
and say *what have we done.*
I could hold you,
say *you are not my son,*
hold you,
tell you lies:

that all babies are born, as you are,
bound to breathing machines,
their bodies small enough to fit a hand
and weighing less than two pounds

that all babies are born equal

that I can look you in the eye

this is no lie:
that the moon of your birth night
tracked your mother
from hospital to hospital
spilled its cool light
on insurance ledgers
weighing your worth

that her fertile heart
froze to sand
each time
she was turned away

that at twenty,
I was a nurse
starched and stupid with notions
of night sirens
unloading pain
at emergency room doors
as call to care

I hold you, Joshua, in my palm,
your chest blows
the breathing machine
and the walls of my denial
tumble

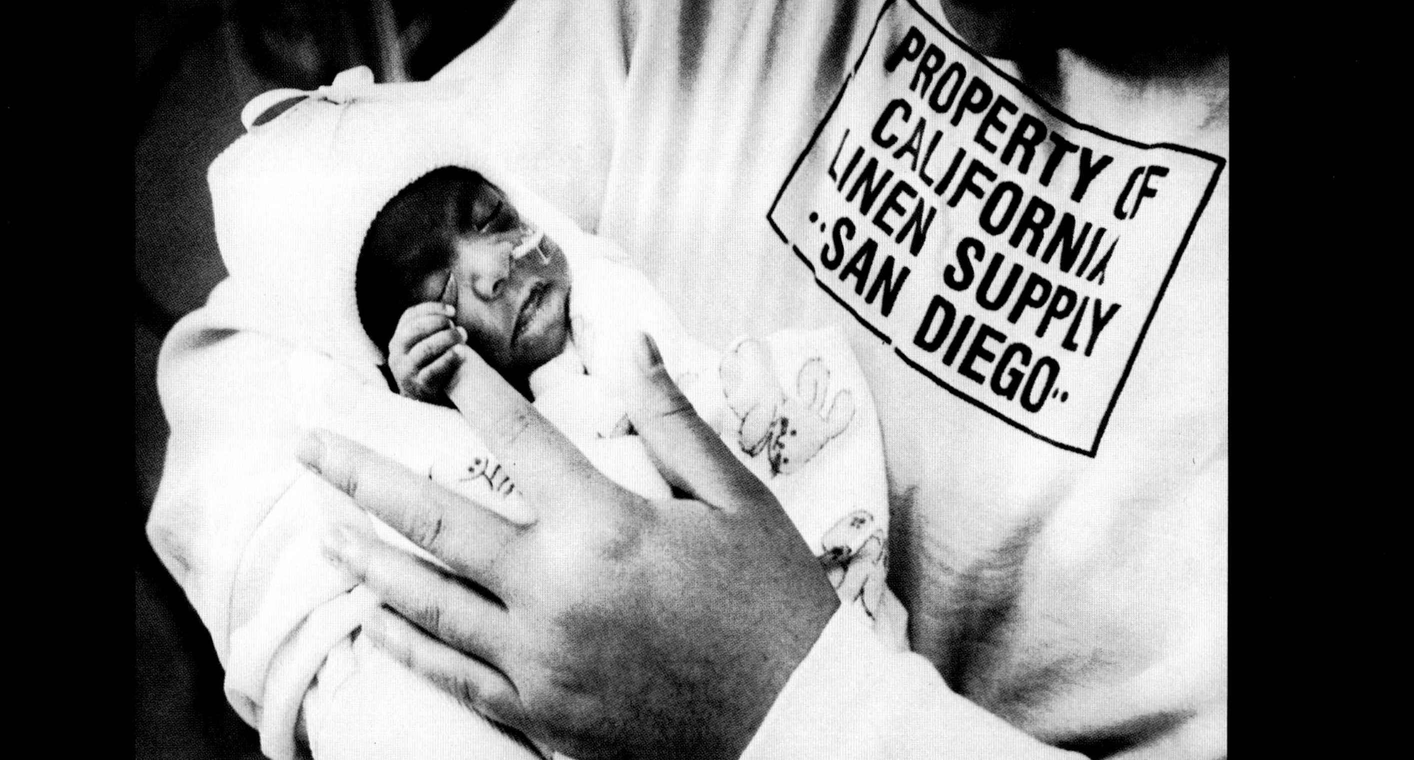

PROPERTY OF
CALIFORNIA
LINEN SUPPLY
"SAN DIEGO"

Umbilicus

inside
the nursery
for intensive
care

the steady
beep beep
 beep beep
of machine
after machine
surrounds me,
surrounds
the incubator

my body knows
which one

*baby
I want to touch
you*

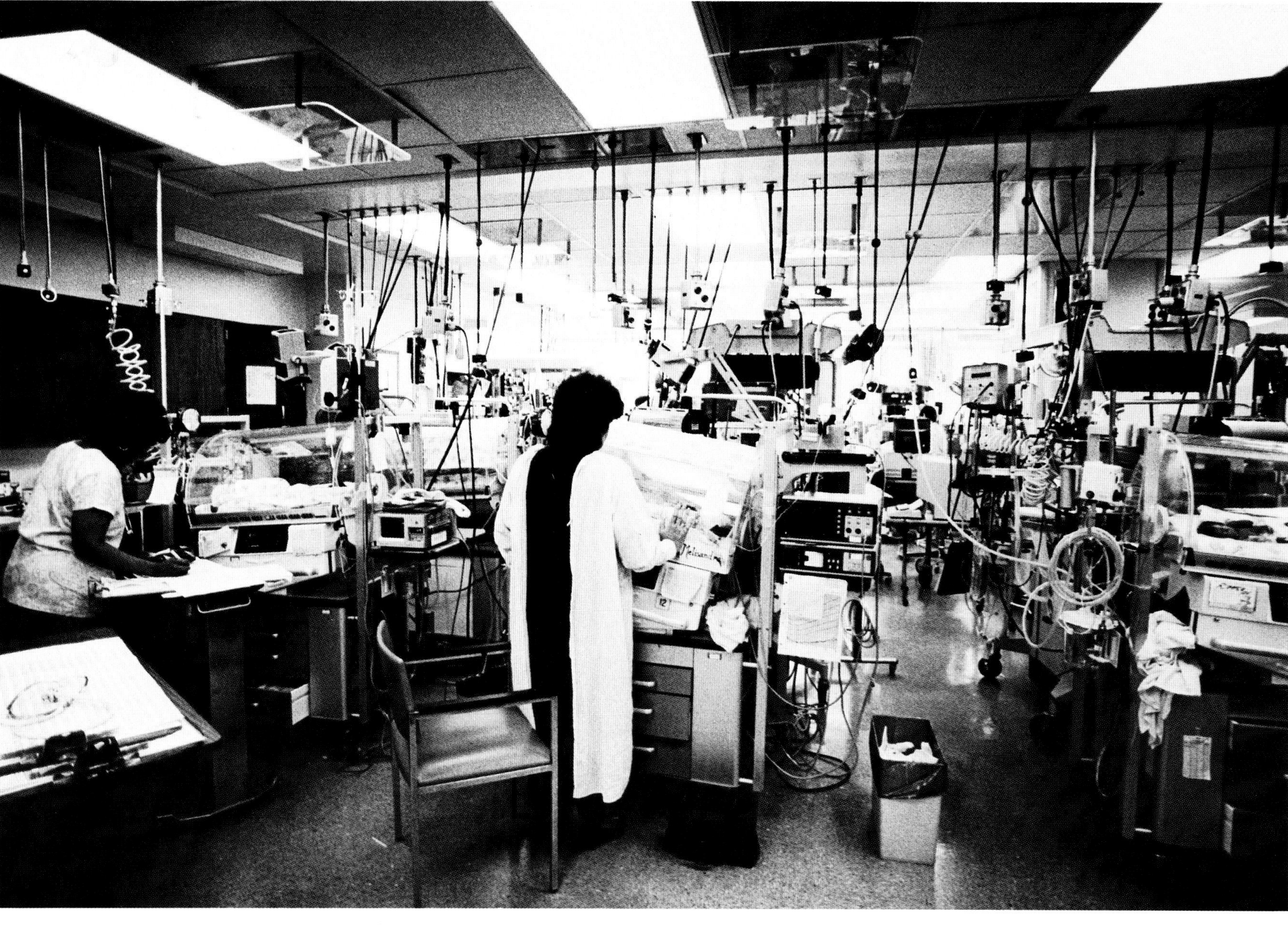

I float
my fingers
on the glass

it is warm
like blood

*what is this
current
between us
pulling me,
reclaiming
my body*

*a thick black
cord
hangs from the ceiling,
plugs
into you,
into my hand*

*am I here
in the nursery*

*or inside
my own womb*

A Little Noise

In San Luis Potosi,
my first boy was born
in the doctor's home
four blocks from my house,
my friends
in the room with me,
my mom mixing the wrong words
to songs under her breath,
my mother-in-law
beside the curtains
twisting her hands,
four sisters-in-law,
my husband, my uncle

In San Diego,
when I have two months and a half
my husband say, go look for care.
I go to Mid-City Clinic, I go
through the glass doors.
I ask them, can you tell me
who can take my care?
And they say, no, I don't think so,
we have too many women

I go to the Chicano Clinic, the woman
with my eyes in her eyes,
she say, come in one week,
I go next week, they have no room

At the Samahan Clinic,
she say, call me again in two months.
In two months, I arrive to the clinic
and nothing

Last month, I go to Ocean View Clinic,
no, she can't take my baby and me
because I have more than four months

I hear a little noise
here in my throat

Who can take my care?

Just wait, the nurse tells me.
When your time comes,
take a taxi, go
to the emergency room

Labored Breathing

All night she can't breathe,
she can't sleep.
All night she walks the kitchen,
rattles the pots.
A child, swelling with child,
her third.
All night she drinks hot water,
her chest fills.

In San Diego, four months
to third birth,
she walks the kitchen,
a little noise swells
in her throat.

In the taxi, windows fish for air.
Emergency room, ice white light,
her chest her world.
A nurse close to her face.
Doctors, the rattle of needles.
The small *beep beep* of the baby's
heartbeat monitored on a machine.

Asthma, the chart reads,
from the Greek
asma, to blow,
labored breathing,
a sense of swelling,
of constriction
in the chest.

Morning, in a hospital bed,
she shows me her photograph,
shot five years ago:
a girl, sixteen years,
in blue jeans,
corn tall behind her,
sunflowers and four months
between her and first birth.

The curtain twists.
The wrong words shuffle
the songs of birth.

A woman
can't breathe in the night,
birth water in her throat.

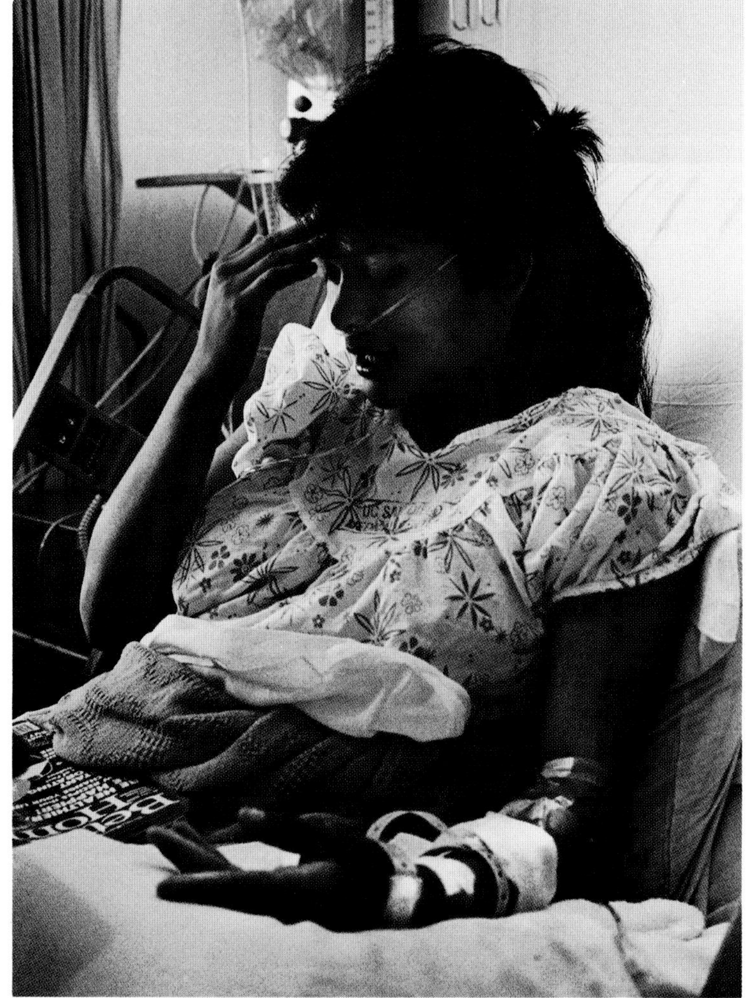

Not Fair

I don't take women
with Medi-Cal insurance
for obstetrics. I have
a note posted in my office
to the effect that I don't feel
that I can provide
the quality of care
that I feel I have to provide
for the kind of reimbursement
I get from Medi-Cal.

And I don't feel
that I can increase my charges
to private patients
to make up for that.
I don't think it's fair.

Obstetrician
June, 1987

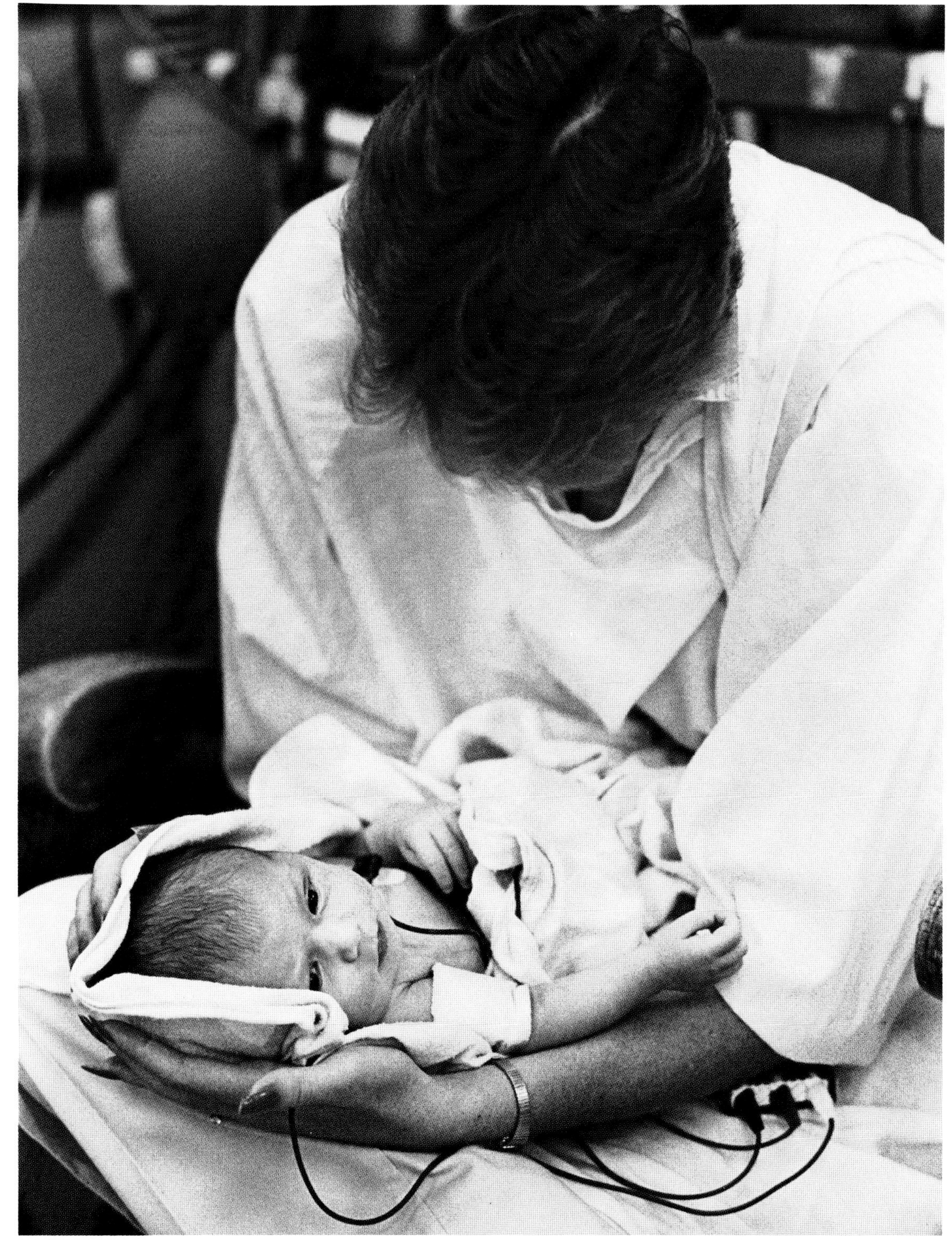

Modern Medicine

This malpractice insurance business
might make me quit medicine,
go back to Haiti, where I was born
and grew up, or to Mexico,
where I went to medical school,
lived a few years.

I remember one evening,
in a little town outside Mazatlan,
a father came to me, knocked on my door,
*please, would you climb onto my tractor,
come, please, my wife, my baby.*
The *curandera,* the midwife,
had sent him.

We drove three hours into night hills,
black tractor smoke filled my lungs.
I could see the shadow of the stable,
smell the horses, pigs, cows.
In the house, a small kerosene lamp
ran light across the bed,
the mother, sweat on her face.

We talked. I examined her.
Her cervix dilated ten centimeters,
the baby's head at zero station.
No membranes.
The contractions are ten minutes apart,
the *curandera* said. Where to hang the IV?
The father found a long rope,
threw it over the beam
running the roof.

Pitocin, to strengthen the uterus,
and four hours later, a healthy baby,
a son. A trembling father
held the flashlight while I sewed.
They paid me with a chicken.

There, the doctor is well respected,
the patient feels *the doctor
is going to do his or her best for me*,
the patients feels *if something happens,
it's because it has to happen.*

And here? Nothing happens
and they still sue you,
some freak accident of nature, a defect,
and they hold me responsible.
They want me to be God
and I'm not.

This year, I'm paying $40,000
a year for malpractice insurance.
It goes up twenty percent a year.
Let's say in five years, I have to pay
$80,000 a year. I don't double my fees
to cover my costs. I would have to see
more and more patients.
And one thing I won't do is practice
shove-push medicine.
You know, take the patient,
and then just say,
Hi. O.K. See you.
And then, *Bye.*
Five minutes,
out the door.
That's not my way,
my approach to medicine.
I'd rather leave,
go back to Haiti, to Mexico,
be paid a chicken.

Pobrecita

Late afternoon sunlight
filters the screen door.
Ana Maria sits on the couch,
both daughters on her lap,
all three in Sunday best dress.
The iron still out on the table.
Emiliana, the baby, six months,
spits, shrieks, smiles,
plays with her doll.
Ana Maria holds Rafaela's head up,
strokes her, murmurs
pobrecita.

Whenever I think about it now,
I remember everything and feel ugly.
How could this happen to me,
to my daughter?

When I first found out I was pregnant,
we didn't have the money
the clinic was charging.
My husband was out of work,
had been in an accident.
I was working in an office
filling out forms. In exchange for that,
when I was six months pregnant,
I could see their doctor on Fourth Avenue.

I saw him three times.
He came in in a white coat, said hello,
touched my stomach,
said everything was fine
and left the room.

Each visit lasted less than five minutes.
He was out the door
before I could ask
why was I so large?
Was I going to have twins?
Was there something wrong?

When I was seven months pregnant,
I had a pain in the top of my stomach.
I couldn't walk, I couldn't breathe.

The doctor touched my stomach,
said everything was fine.
But I knew something was wrong.
I went home, called the clinic,
please, would you see me,
my doctor isn't listening to my pain.

That doctor is a good doctor,
the nurse at the clinic told me,
go back, see him.

A week later, Rafaela was born,
She was blue.

Hypoxia, deficiency of oxygen,
the doctor would write later
in the chart. Polyhydramnios,
increased amniotic fluid,
a signal the fetus sends.

The doctor took her out, wiped her face,
sucked her throat with a tube,
placed her on my stomach.

I saw she was not moving,
asked what was wrong.
He told me *she needs oxygen,*
handed her to his assistant, left the room.
I never saw him again.

For fifteen days, a machine
breathed for her. She had seizures,
not enough oxygen when she was inside me.
They didn't know if she would live.
They told me *she may not breathe*
on her own, ever.

They asked me, like a door slamming shut,
do you want us to remove her
from the machine?

For fifteen days,
I watched the breathing machine
push her chest up and down.
I prayed. And I prayed.
She began to breathe on her own.

The doctor says she has brain damage
but I know she's getting better.
She knows me. She makes sounds. She
screams.

Sometimes I get angry.
If he had just taken more time,
watched for signals.
He never weighed me, checked my blood.
If he had listened to that pain,
maybe he could've done something.
But he was rough, too much in a hurry.

I remember after Rafaela was born,
he didn't freeze me when he sewed me.
It hurt, hurt more than the birth.
I screamed
but he kept right on sewing
as if I were a cow
or a donkey.

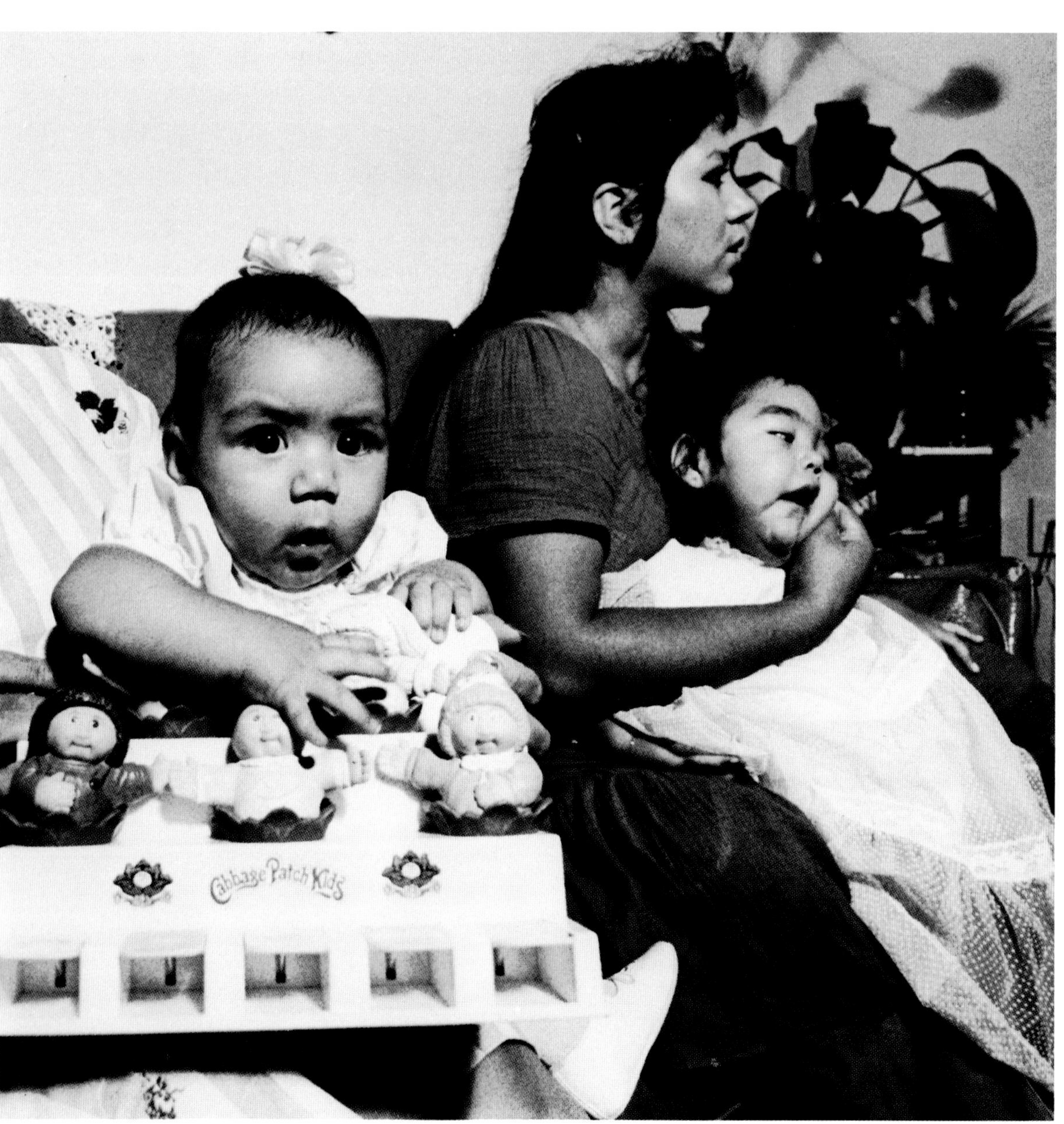

Emiliana

Everything was different
when Emiliana was born.
They saw me at the clinic
every month for the first few months,
then every week after that.
They weighed me, checked my blood,
the baby's heartbeat, and mine,
watched her move on a screen.

They told me *drink milk, eat meat,
vegetables, fish. Take vitamins.
Call if you have pain, call if you bleed.*

Once, I went for a test
for sugar in my blood,
had to go without breakfast.
The doctor asked *did I feel weak,
did I want to lie down.*
He cared, he cared how I felt.

They made sure I saw a specialist.
I was afraid it might happen again.
She checked everything about Rafaela,
told me it was not my genes.
She spoke to that doctor.
He said it might have been his fault,
but it could have been
something else too,
and to know what had happened
was impossible.

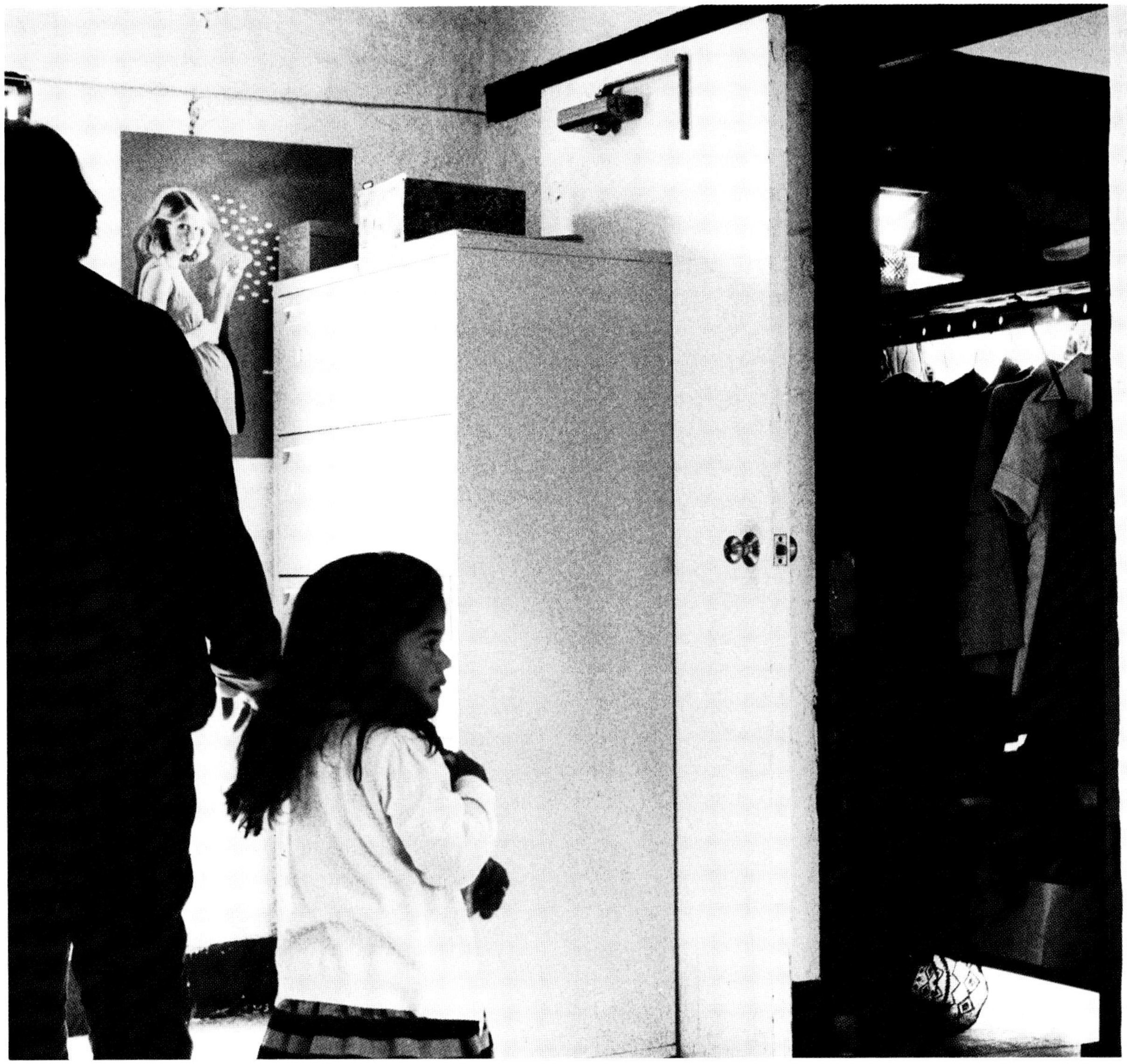

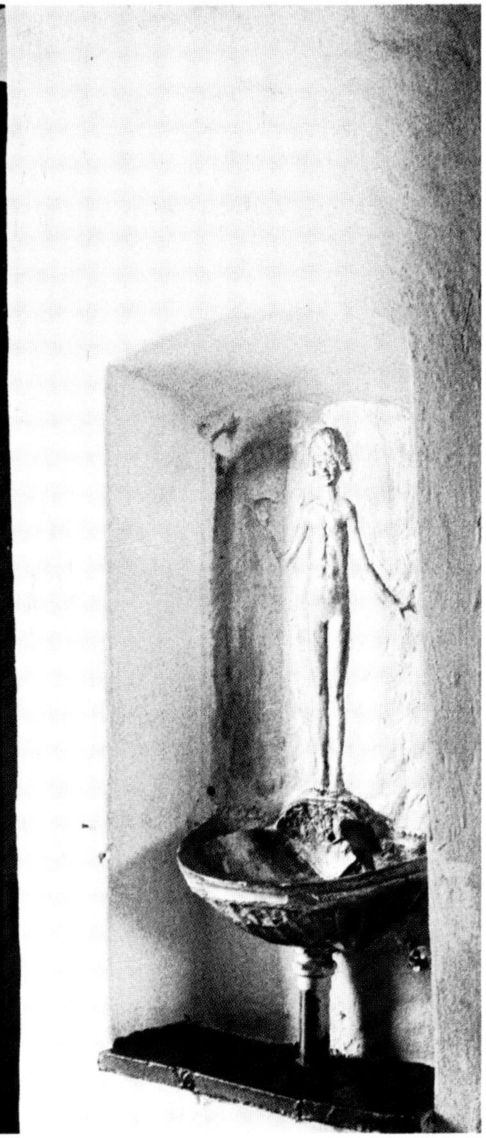

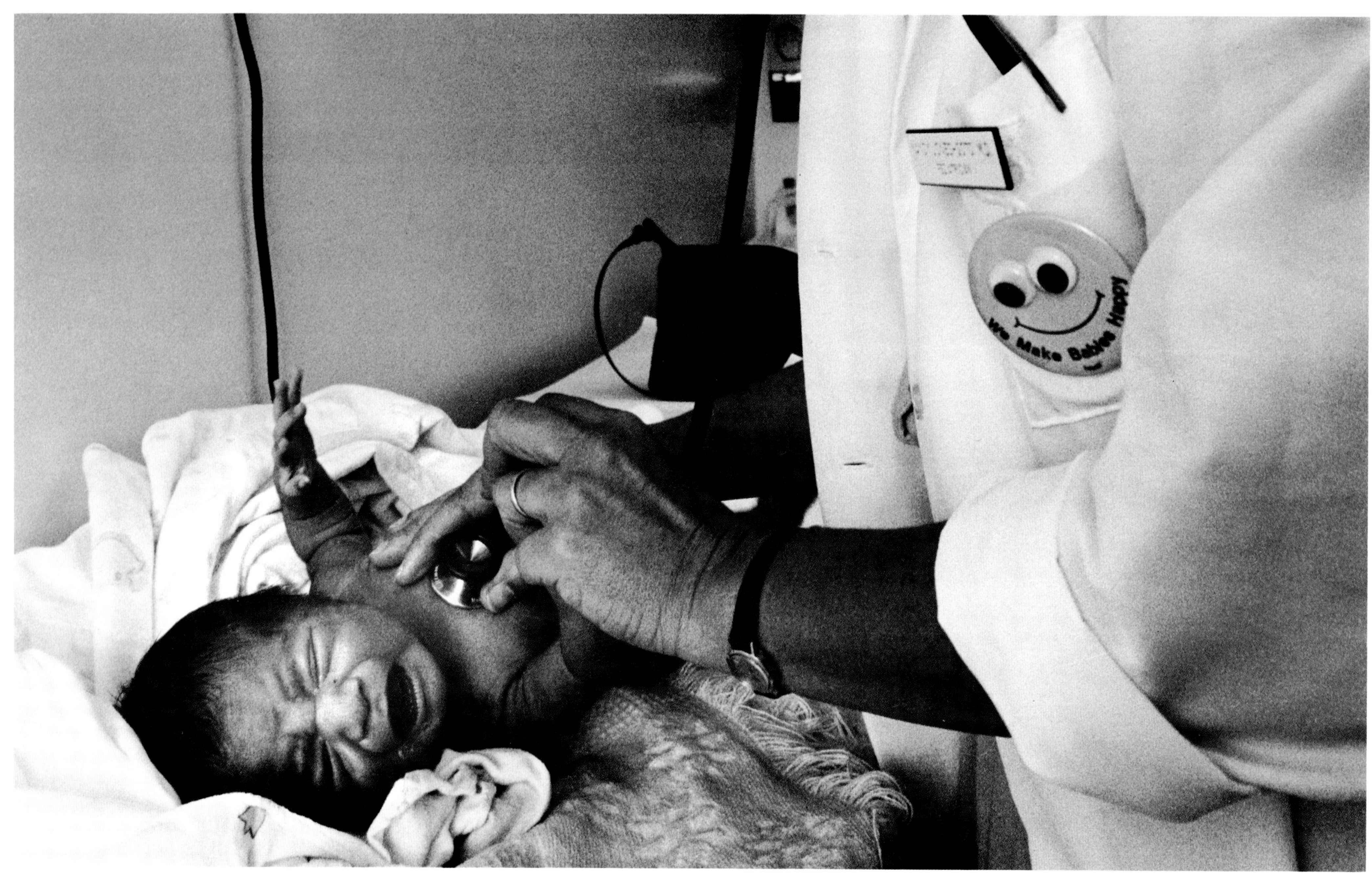

We Make Babies Happy

Clinic: No Vacancy

We can accept only 100 women a month into our thirteen-clinic program, limited by the number of deliveries our hospital can take.

In January 1987 alone, we had to turn away more than 600 women.

If we could contract with more physicians to deliver patients, we could take more women.

— Ann Bush, Director, Comprehensive Perinatal Program, University of California, San Diego, Medical Center, prototype for the State of California

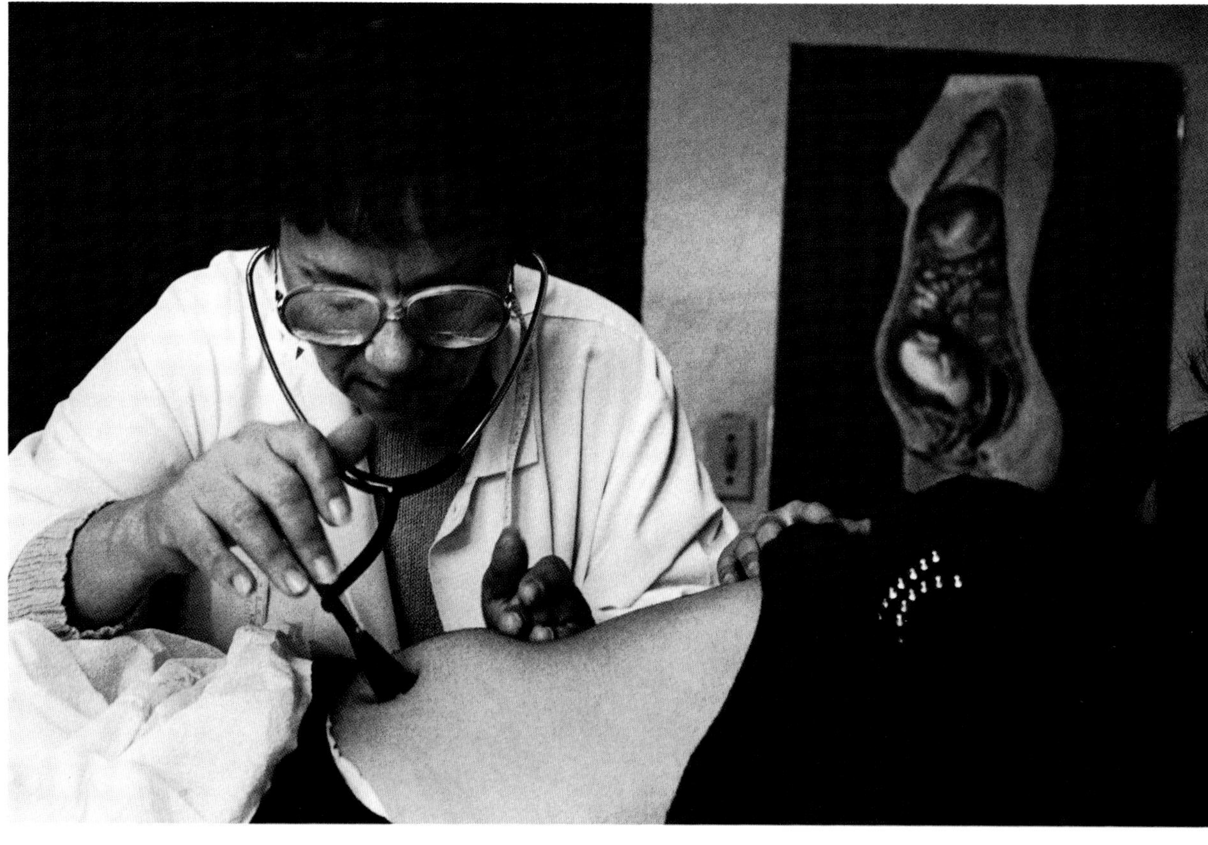

*Back
to a time
when women faced death
at each birth.*

*How soon, my Dear, death may my steps attend,
How soon't may be thy lot to lose thy friend,*

poet Anne Bradstreet wrote to her husband
in the late seventeenth century
before the birth of one of her children.

In the late twentieth century,
a woman in labor
on a railroad track
dressed in socks and a polo shirt
and nothing else.

A thirteen year old child
with stomach cramps
in the emergency room.
In labor? Pregnant?
Her parents,
living with her for nine months,
did not know.

A black woman lies on a stretcher
in hospital in labor.
She lived in the alley
until last week
when St. Vincent de Paul shelter
opened, gave her a bed.

Anne Bradstreet,
poor women
have not come so far
these 300 years.

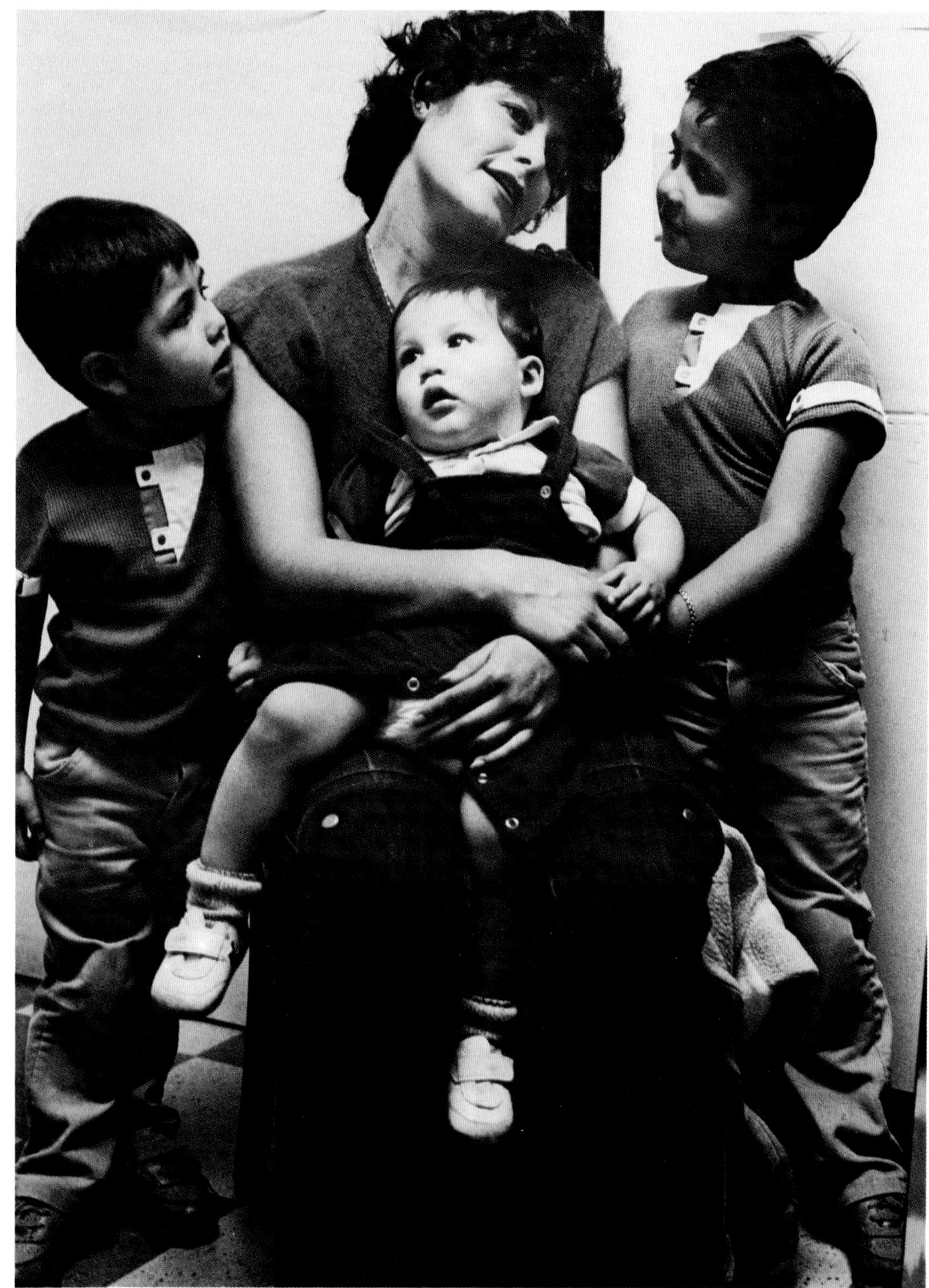

Birth song

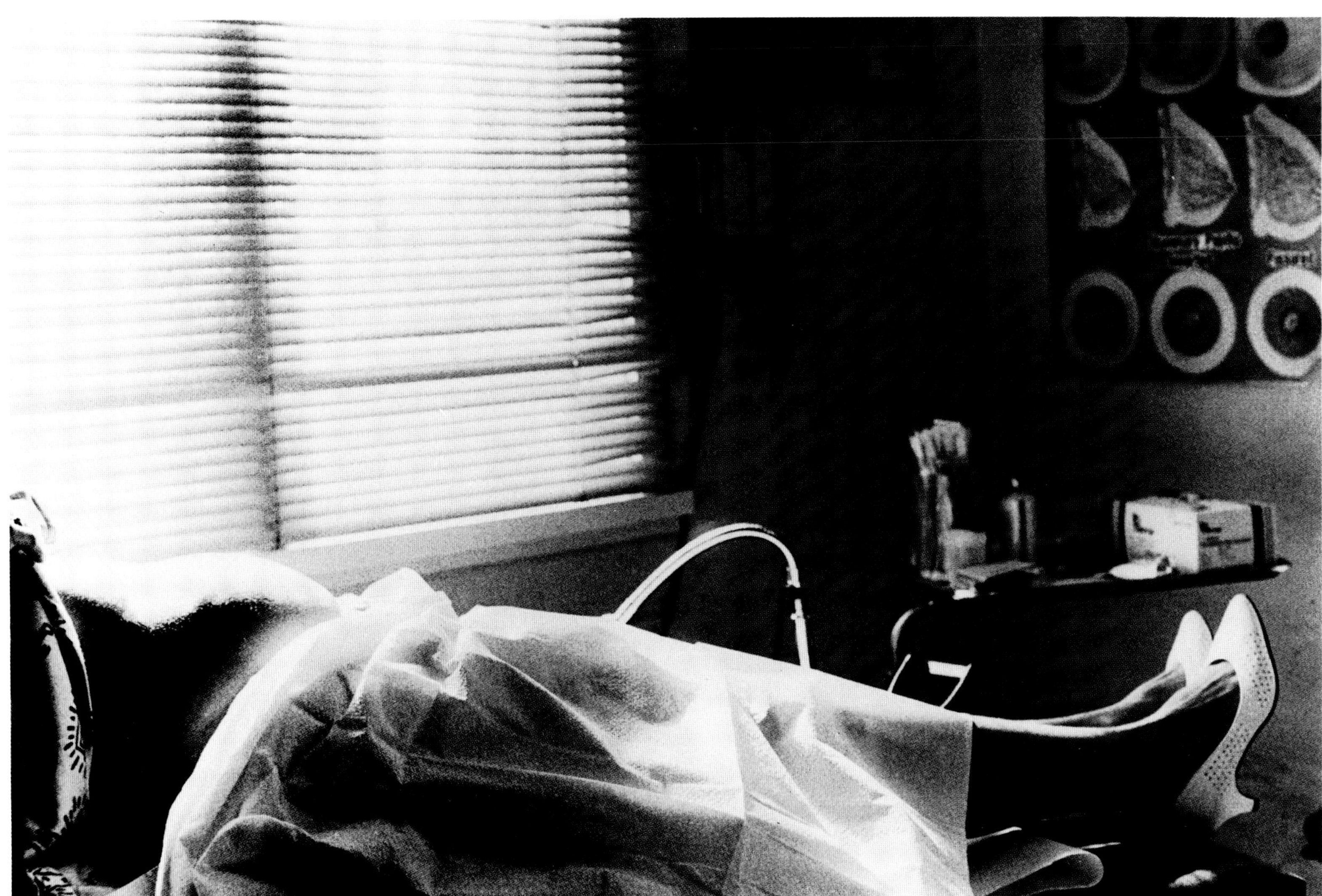

Changing

When I trained in the seventies
obstetrics was changing
from a basically male-oriented,
male-dominated specialty,
to an era that I liked so much,
in which women were being looked at
as more than just simply individuals
who were taking part in some event.
I think prior to the 1970s,
it was very mechanical.

Women and women's opinions
in regard to what their birth
and what their pregnancy should be about
was of secondary
or maybe non-importance.

Hard To Handle

Did I ever see a doctor
before my babies were born?
Go on, I would never think of a thing like that.
But I had a doctor deliver my babies,
all of them, all of them at home.

Back in ranch country in Walden, Colorado,
where *I* was born,
must have been eighteen ninety-eight,
now *they* would never see a doctor,
not for a delivery, not for no time at all.
I remember when my brother was born,
Gramma and Mrs. Peterson
took care of Momma,
delivered the baby.

I remember it was hayin' time,
wild hay, different than your alfalfa.
I didn't work the fields yet,
too little, only nine at the time.
I used to run the water
for the sickle grinder.
Sickles had to be ground, kept sharp

for the mowers. Wild hay's
hard to cut, hard to handle.

My Gerald, my first child,
was born at home in Bowie,
Bowie, Colorado, a minin' town.
My husband was a miner.
I remember the doctor
spilled the ether,
upset it in the bed beside me,
was that a mess.
It deadened my whole body,
slowed things down some.
Gerald was born in August,
s'posed to be born in September.
He didn't have his toenails
or his fingernails. But he was strong,
weighed nine pounds, ten ounces.
I never had a baby baby.

My Anna weighed twelve pounds, six ounces.
That's when I had milk-leg.
This leg swelled as big as my waist,
looked like if you touched it, it would pop.
In those days, they didn't know
what to do for it.
I laid in bed for months.

I worked in the fisheries
over in San Pedro
when I first came to California
in nineteen twenty-seven.
I ground the knives,
kept them sharp for boning.
Two years later, Norma came.
For nine months, bless her heart,
she was a wild woman
inside me. When her time came,
she was born on the dinin' room table.
Yeah, they wouldn't do
what I told them to do.
I told them if they'd just
reach up there
and release that bone, my tail bone?

It's bent, you know, it's crooked.
Instead of whippin' us kids,
Papa never whipped,
but that boot of his
could work pretty hard.
All they had to do
was to bear that bone down
and the baby would have been there.
I suffered hours for that.

The baby should've been born
hours before that,
should've been born
around nine or ten o'clock,
that's when she should've been born.
And she would've been,
if they'd 've done
what I told them to do,
if they'd 've been sharp.

Almost Outside

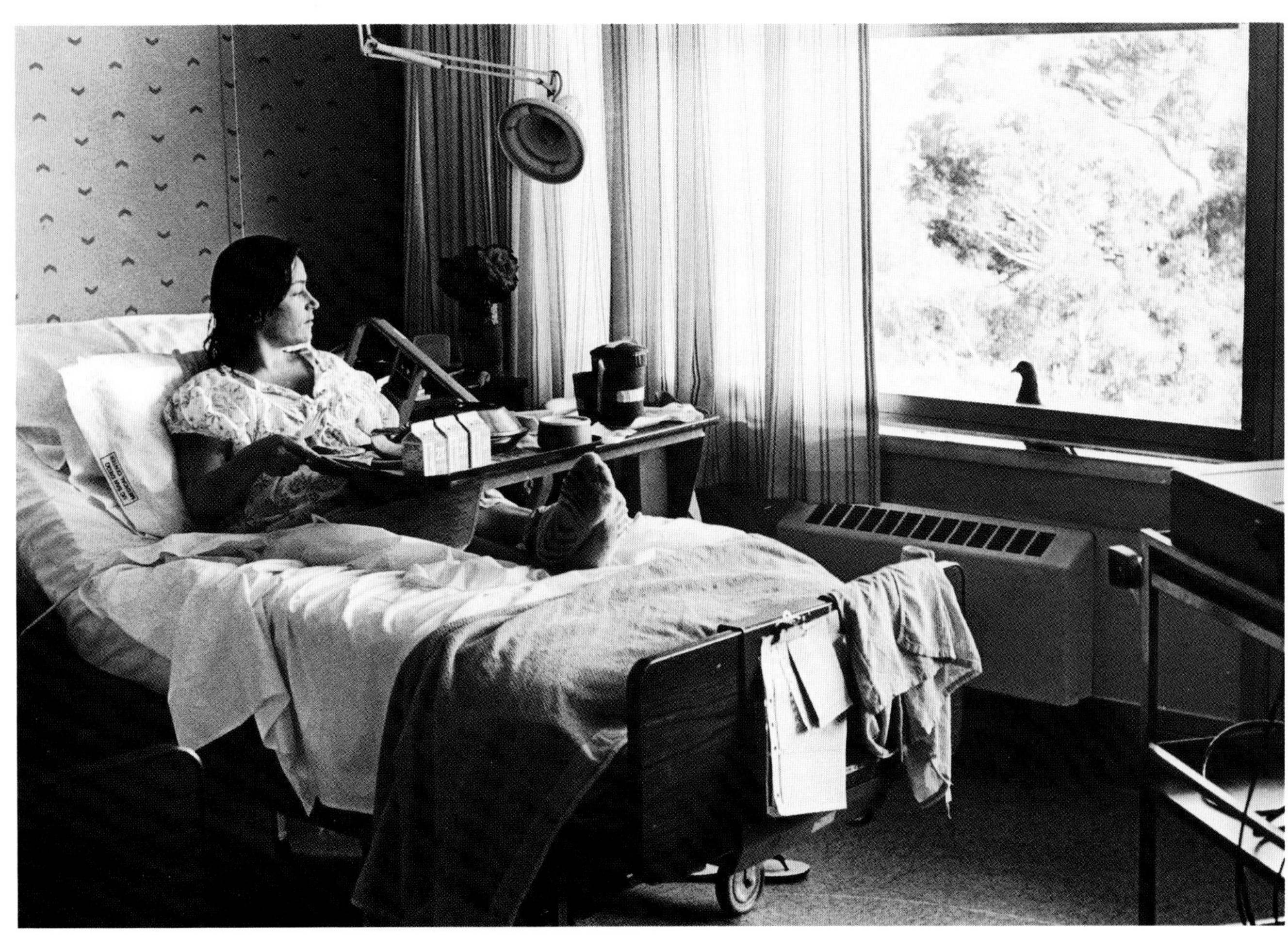

The pigeon perches everyday
on the hospital window ledge.
After I feed him
small chunks of bread,
he waits, doesn't fly away.
He wears a green band
around his leg,
he's been tagged,
he's been homed.
At the jail,
when they found out I was pregnant,
they put a red band
around my leg
instead of a blue one
so they'd know not to bodyslam me
up against the wall.

I was in jail
for trying to steal someone's purse
from a grocery store.
The day after I was locked inside,
I said *thank God it's over.*
I don't have to run anymore.
When I get out
I can go get a job,
and praise God,
begin a new life for myself,
my daughter, my new baby.

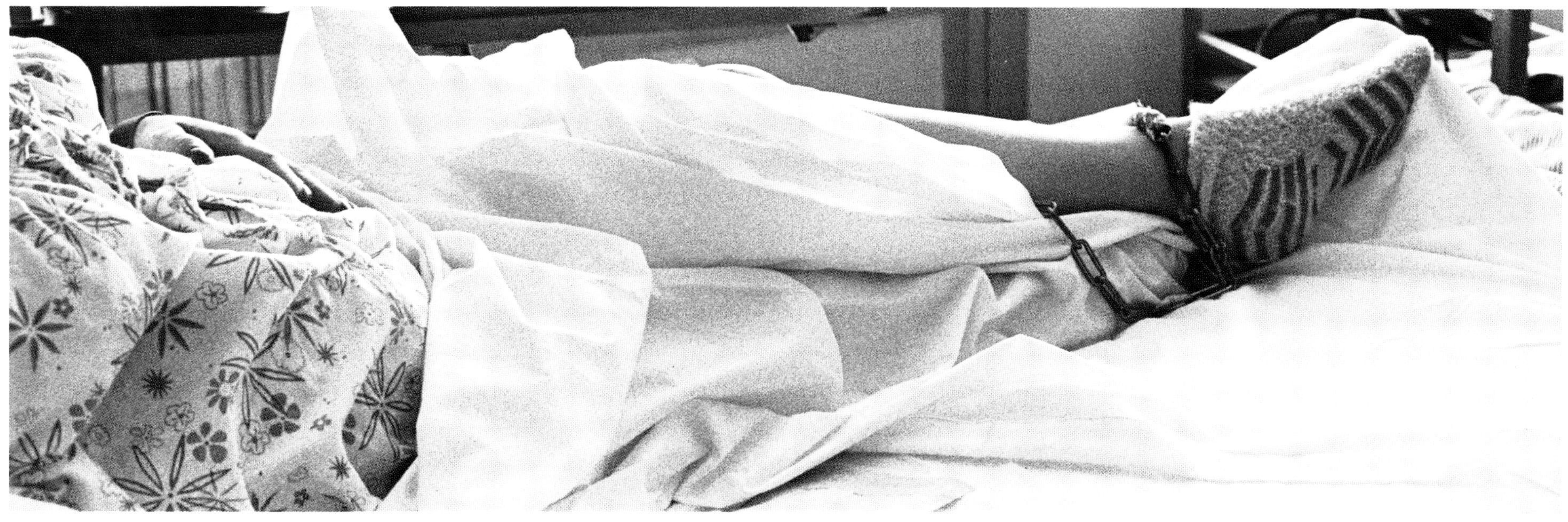

I was six months pregnant,
sleeping in an eight by eleven foot
cement cell on the floor,
with three inmates who smoked,
the window sealed shut.
and a three inch steel door.
The blower fan in the ceiling
spun dead air,
the walls began to sweat.
I could feel my baby break
open, water run down my legs.
That's when they brought me
to hospital, told me my son
was struggling to be born.
You need rest, it is too soon.

They put me next to the window,
next to the trees, the air,
almost outside.
The jail sent a guard.
He snapped a steel chain around my ankle,
locked me to the bed.
I could feel my son move inside me.
He waits,
on the edge of his eighth month,
his small lungs
folded like wings.

A Hate For Heroin

I was desperate for drugs
when I tried it.
Not any more, no way.
I don't care how bad it gets,
I'll never, please God, go back to that.
You thinks it takes away all your fears,
your cares, takes away the guilt
of not living up to yourself.
But it takes away nothing, only deadens.
You don't really know what's going on.
You think you do, you think you're joe cool,
but you're really just a nothing.
I have a horrible hate for heroin.
It's lost its little treasure.
I know what it did to me
and to my new daughter.
Christ has taken away
my desire for it.
Now I have my highs
with God
and my family.

"I am the sweat of a stranger's child in fever ..."

- from "*Mother Tongue*"

waking from worry

his small bottom
fits exactly
the hollow
of my hand,
hollow all my life
waiting
for what belonged to it

I wasn't nervous
when he was born,
just shaking,
my body waking
from worry I carried
nine months
before he was born,
worry I carried
like a jagged chain
growing inside me,
carried to work
sticking and gnawing
inside me,
carried it days I cooked
at one restaurant,
then nights I cooked at another,
carried it gnawing two jobs
no insurance
not enough money for a doctor,
two jobs

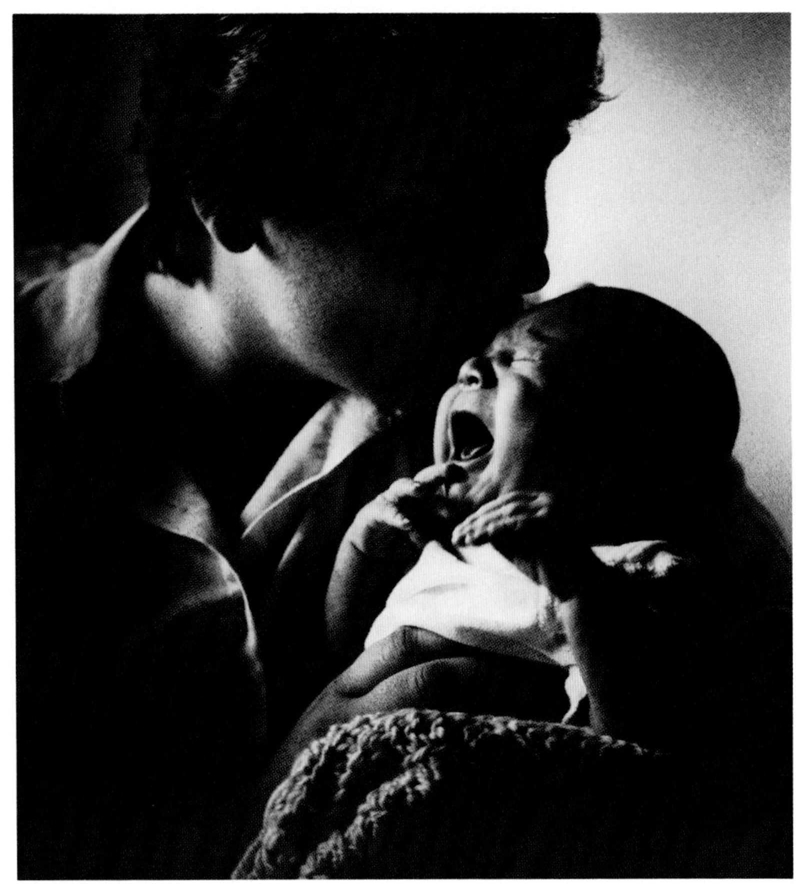

and my wife
eighteen,
carrying our baby
through halls at Granite Hills High
heavy with worry,
both her uncles born handicapped,
a chain I'd carry forever
what if something goes wrong

my son was born a month early,
his skin yellow, his liver
immature but ok,

the relentless chain snapped open,
it disappeared from my gut

he came out
all balled up, not crying,
then scared, surprised at his freedom
cried when he found he could move
stretch out his legs, his arms

he quieted only when I held him
here
in the hollow
of my hand

her daughter's cheek
tight
as a kiss
against her arm

she tried
to take care of her
before she was born,
went to the clinic
but they couldn't
see her

their doctor
had resigned

no insurance company
would cover
him
to see her
or any women
at the clinic

why do they think
he needs to cover himself,
spread insurance money
like leaves
over his arms, his legs,

does he need
some special kind of armor,
a shield,
to protect him
from her

protect him
from whom?

a woman
named Rhonda Sue

born in El Cajon,
who went to Grossmont High

her husband
works

too many hours
for too little money

and no insurance

were they expecting
a warrior?

All The People

I once saw a bumper sticker.
Send your son to medical school, it said.
Support my son the lawyer.
Those are fighting words.

For two years I fought,
flew to Washington
with other obstetricians
to lobby our senators
and congressmen
about problems we're facing
not only with malpractice
but also with access to care
for pregnant women.

We got nowhere.

We talked to a Senator's aide
about malpractice insurance
and the fact that fewer and fewer
obstetricians
can afford to deliver
babies of poor women.
Thirteen counties in California
don't have OB care
for poor pregnant women.

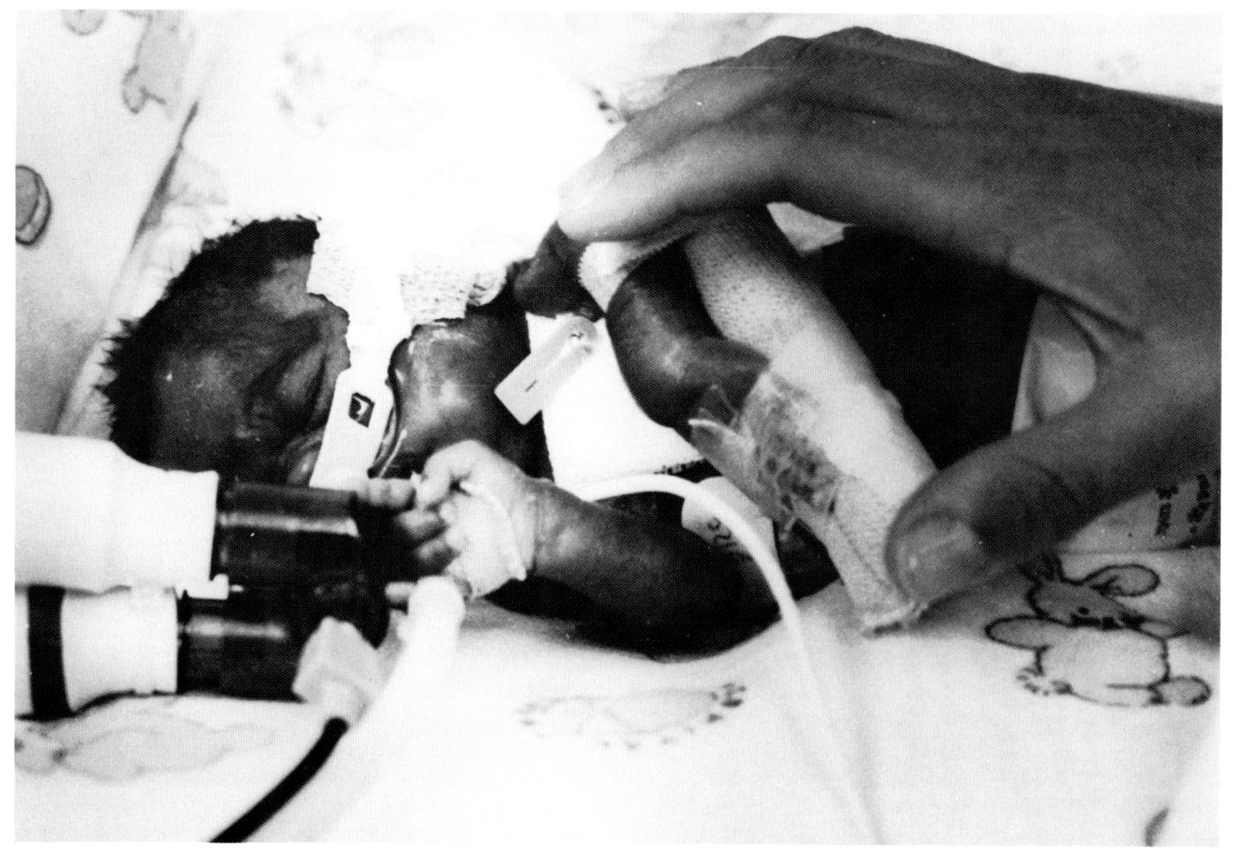

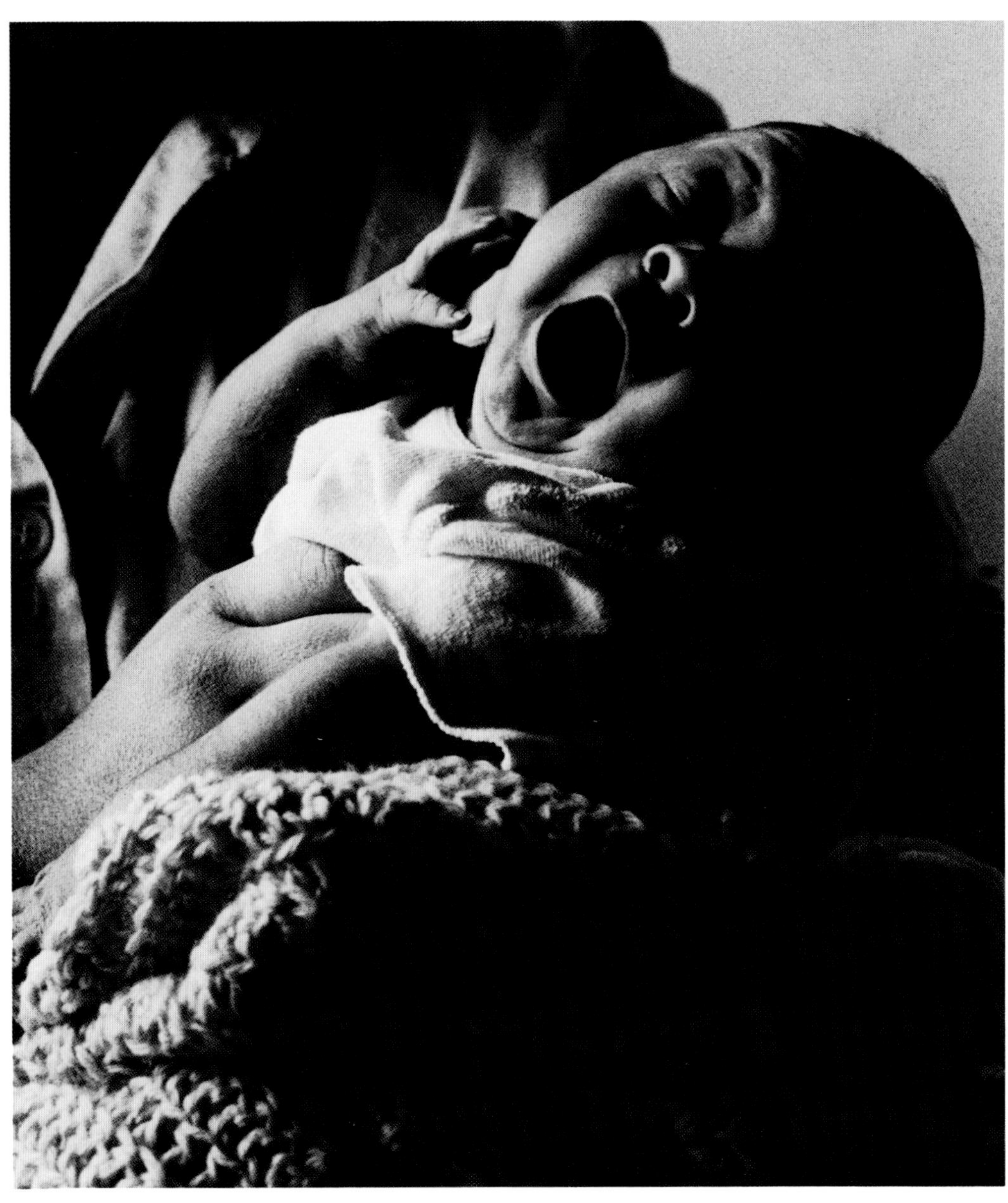

His aide told us,
*We don't perceive this as an issue.
We've not gotten any mail on this
from our constituents.
We have a list of how many
come in on each topic.
We go by the letters we get.*

We went to a Congressman's aide. He told us,
*Right now it's the African issue, race problems.
That's what people are talking about,
so that's what I'm working on.
That's the issue that gives the congressman
the most exposure.*

We asked a Senator,
*Can't we sit down with the lawyers
at a table and talk, work things out?*
He said, *Let's be reasonable.
I'm an attorney and I've got to tell you
there's no incentive at all for an attorney
to come to the bargaining table with you.
You've got to want to gain something.
The attorneys stand to lose,
they stand to lose a lot of money.
The only way doctors and lawyers
will sit down together
is through public pressure.*

You ask about solutions.
I guess I've become cynical.
Solution is always by crisis,
and we're not there yet.
Because welfare patients
can't get OB care
is not a crisis.

Poor women don't make enough noise.
They just come to the emergency room
at high risk with no pre-natal care
and that's terrible.
It seems the crisis will only come
when private patients can't get care.

Today, in Broward County, in Florida,
there's no obstetrical care
available to anyone.
Malpractice rates went up again
forty to fifty percent
to $140,000 a year.
Obstetricians are saying,
*No, we're not going to do it,
we're not doing deliveries anymore.*

Women in that community
—these are private patients—
flew to a meeting of the legislature,
saying, *You've got to do something,
we can't get care!*
And the legislators told them,
We're studying it, we're studying it.

I don't know that I have an answer.
Perhaps a plan is to have
all the people involved
sit down together
and work out a solution:
the attorneys,
the insurance companies,
the physicians,
the government ...

*Obstetrician
September 1987
Former member, malpractice committee
American College of Obstetrics
and Gynecology*

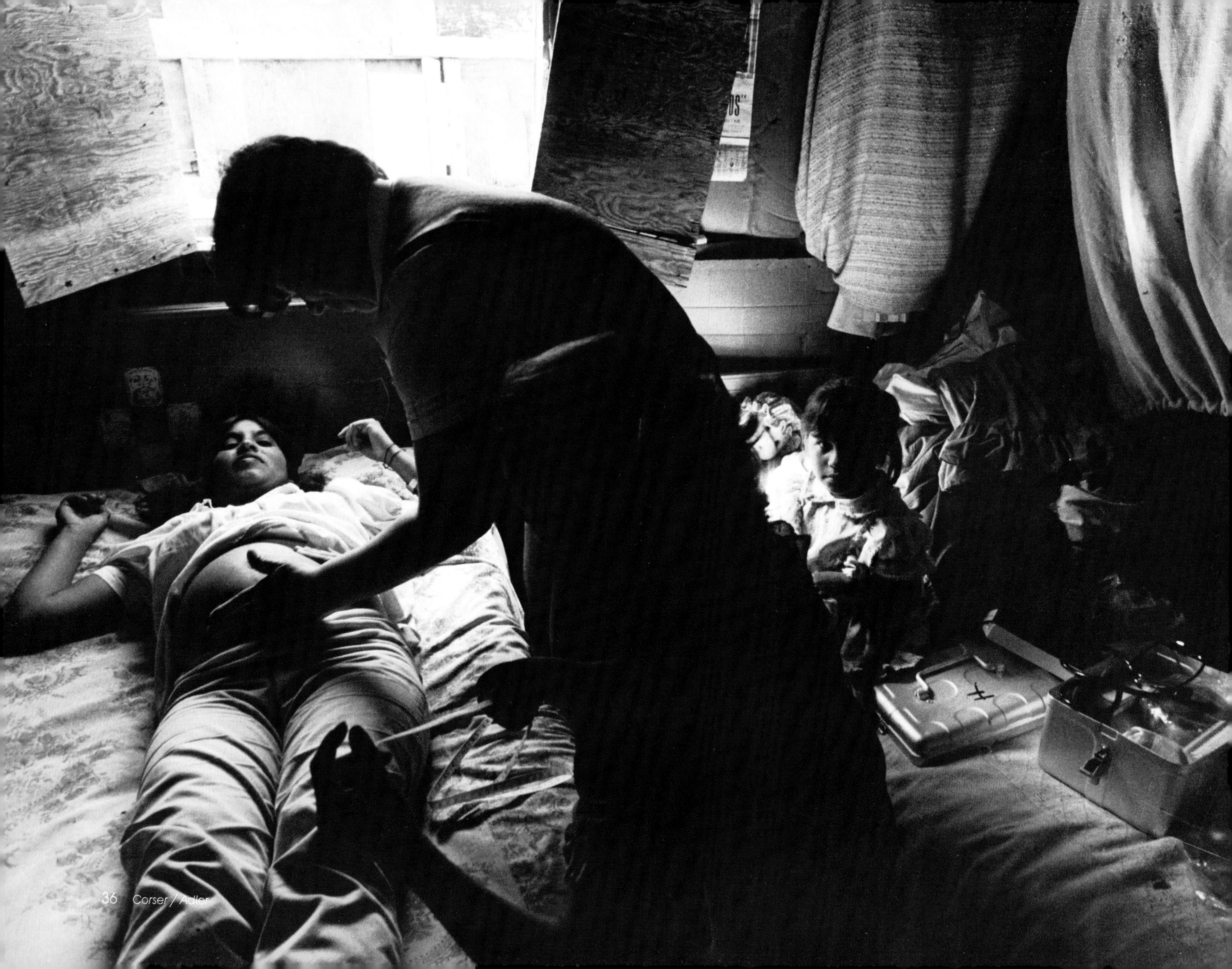
36 Corser / Adler

Around The World

"The issue of providing adequate preventive care for pregnant women in the U.S. is neither medical nor financial. It is political. The means are available to do a better job. Many countries with fewer resources than the U.S. are doing it.

—C. Arden Miller, M.D., professor and chairman, Department of Maternal and Child Health, University of North Carolina at Chapel Hill, from his testimony presented before the Committee on Children, Youth and Families, U.S. Congress, April 28, 1987.

Christine

social worker, Singapore

In Singapore,
because we are a family-oriented society,
if you are pregnant,
you are *the big one*
and everybody tries their best
to take care of you.

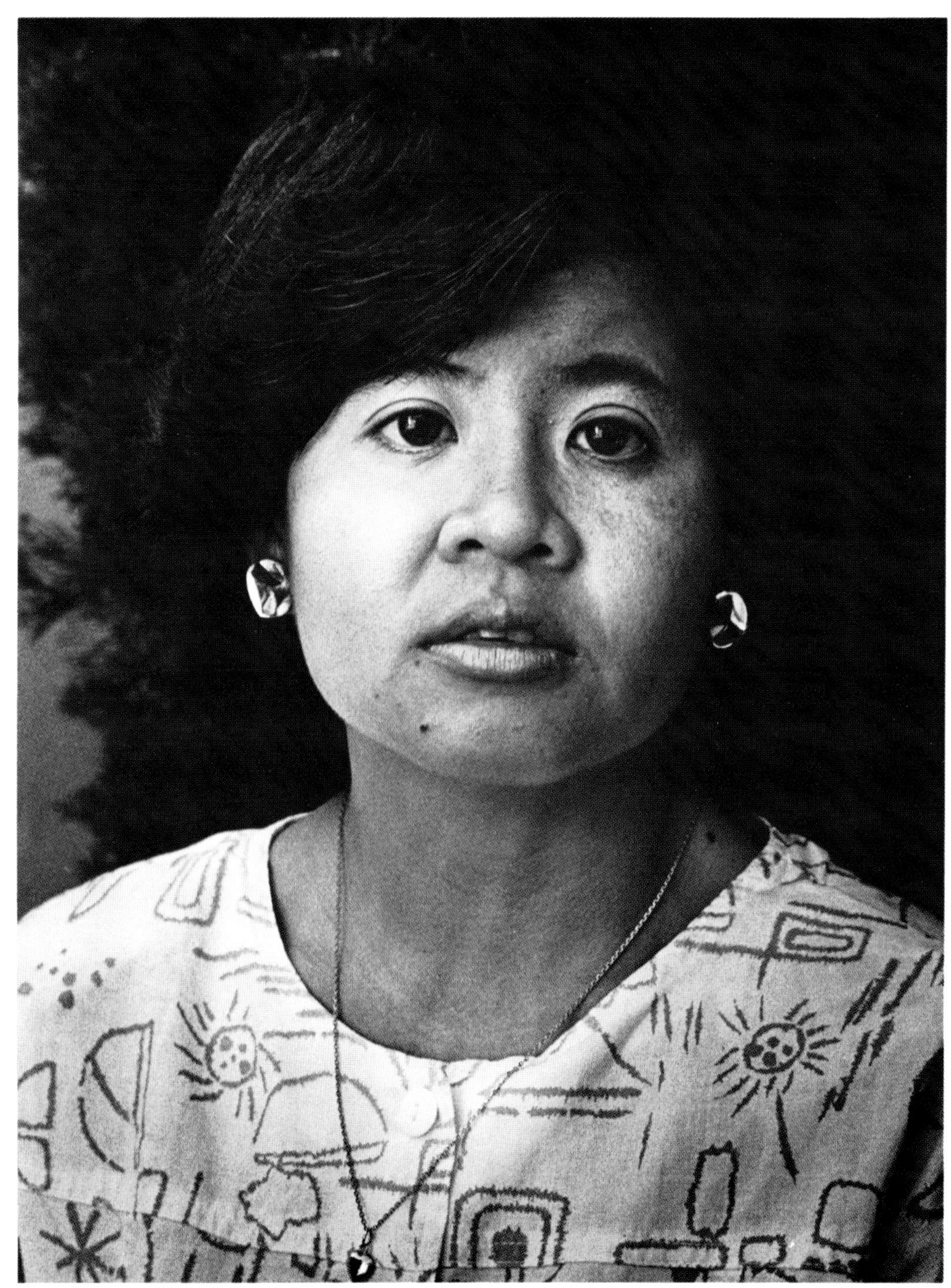

If you don't have any family or friends
or you are very poor,
the government will provide care,
charge you only a little amount of money.

I was so surprised to hear
you have many problems
here in the United States.

Last night, I saw an ad on TV.
A woman is not feeling well,
concerned about an injury she has.
Instead of saying *call this doctor*
someone is saying *call this lawyer.*

I don't really understand
this concept of malpractice medicine.

Maybe one solution
would be to do away
with these legal practices
and that would stop the problems.
I don't understand
why doctors are worried
about malpractice
if they are doing the right thing,
trying to help the patient.

"We should understand that the most economical kind of health expenditure we can make is the one that improves the health and environment of children, from pre-natal life to the time of early schooling. Few medical problems are more underattended than this one ..."

—Dr. Donald Kennedy, professor of biology and president, Stanford University

Isabelle

social worker, France

In France,
the government spends money
to save money,
based on the belief
that a baby born healthy
costs less in the long run.

A pregnant woman
is given incentives
to go for pre-natal care:
if she goes for check-ups
during her pregnancy,
she gets a financial bonus
when her baby is born.
A woman even comes to her home,
helps with the baby
and the shopping
and the housework.

*"After studying 10 European countries—
Belgium, Denmark, France, the Federal Republic
of Germany, Ireland, Netherlands, Norway,
Spain, Switzerland, and the United Kingdom—
it is clear that no pregnant woman in Europe
needs to ask how or where she will receive care
or who will pay for it. In all countries,
perinatal care is either free, without means
testing, or involves negligible charges that are
readily waived in the event of need."*

*—C. Arden Miller, M.D., from his study
"Maternal Health and Infant Survival: An
International Perspective," 1987*

Lise

social worker, Norway

Maternity care is very good
in Norway,
that's for sure.
All pre-natal care and delivery,
everything is free,
absolutely free.
We have nurse midwives
who always deliver the baby
unless there's a complication
and then the doctor helps.

There's no place
that I know of
in Europe
where a pregnant woman
can't get care.

No Room at the Inn

Any woman's death diminishes me.
—Adrienne Rich

Beside the old highway,
a barn.
I have been here before.
I have never been here.

The smell of scattered hay,
slashes of light
like steps across the floor,
the smack of loose wood against wood
in wind.
I am back.

Back
floats
under a screen of memory
out of reach
like some dream
banished with waking.

Morning light
enters roof holes,
fingers an old quilt,

a broken suitcase,
a brush,
tosses particles of hay
like questions
into the air.

A woman has been here,
blood and water,
a birth in the barn.

Birth Light

for Kira

this morning
you photographed,
caught with camera,
the light
of the birth
of a baby

or is it the other way around,
birth light caught you

eighteen years ago
you struggled three days
to bring your son to birth.
and in the night
they put you to sleep
and took the baby from you.
for three days more
(though nothing was wrong)
they would not let you
see him, hold him to your skin
*Where is my son, let me
see my son, something's wrong,
what's wrong, please let me see him.*
it seemed
like you were speaking
a foreign language.
no one would listen.

this morning
the hospital room was soft
like home, you tell me,
like a bedroom in your own home
lights turned down
a windowseat with mauve cushions
a painting of a soaring kite

the doctor's voice was soft
won't be long now
the baby's coming,
her head is crowning
he kidded a bit, cushioned the pain

you walk in, you know,
and there's a woman in labor
and you know what's going to happen
and you see her tummy
and you know what's going to happen
and then

what you know is going to happen
is wiped away
and there's a baby
and it has never happened before

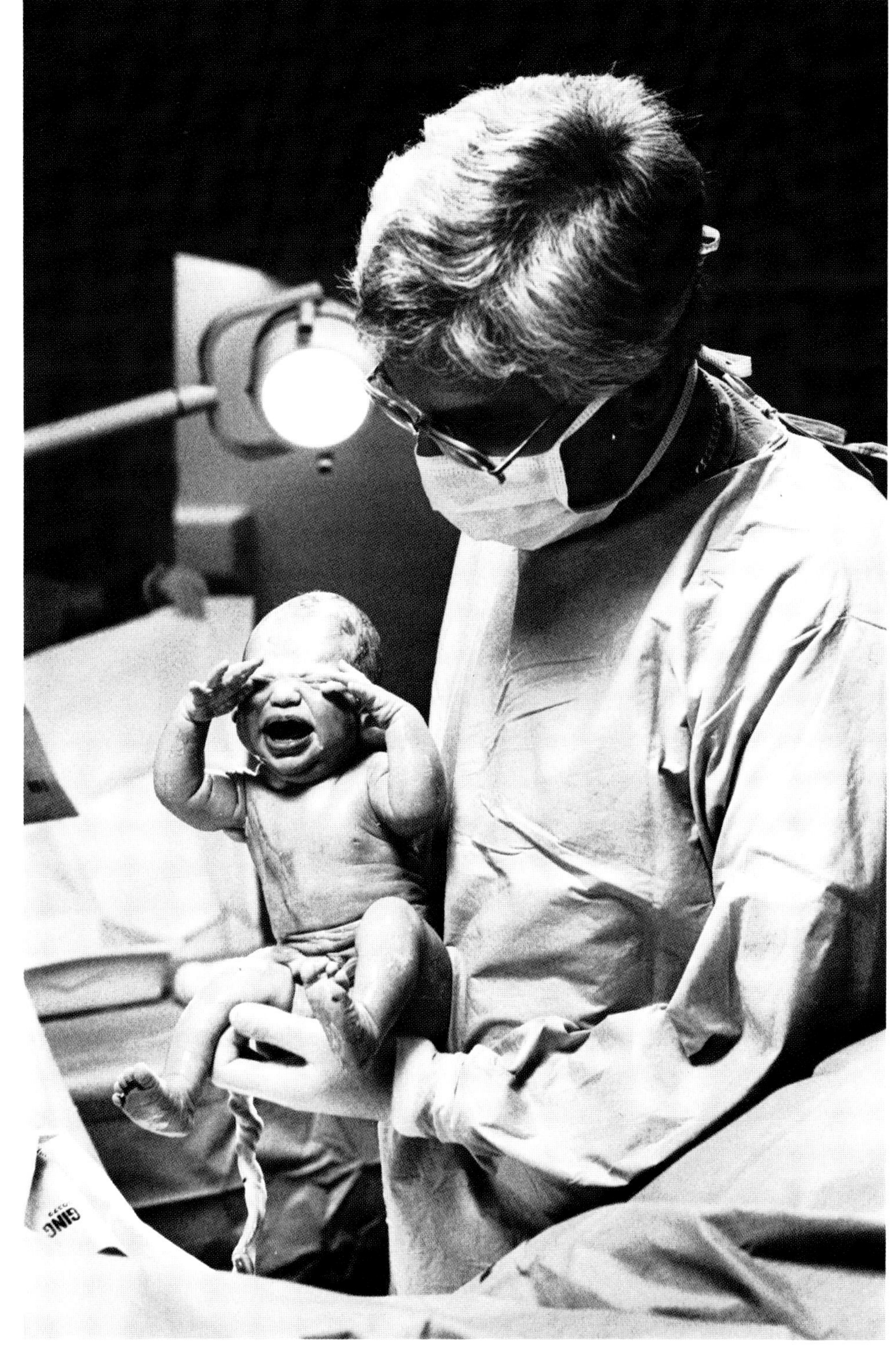

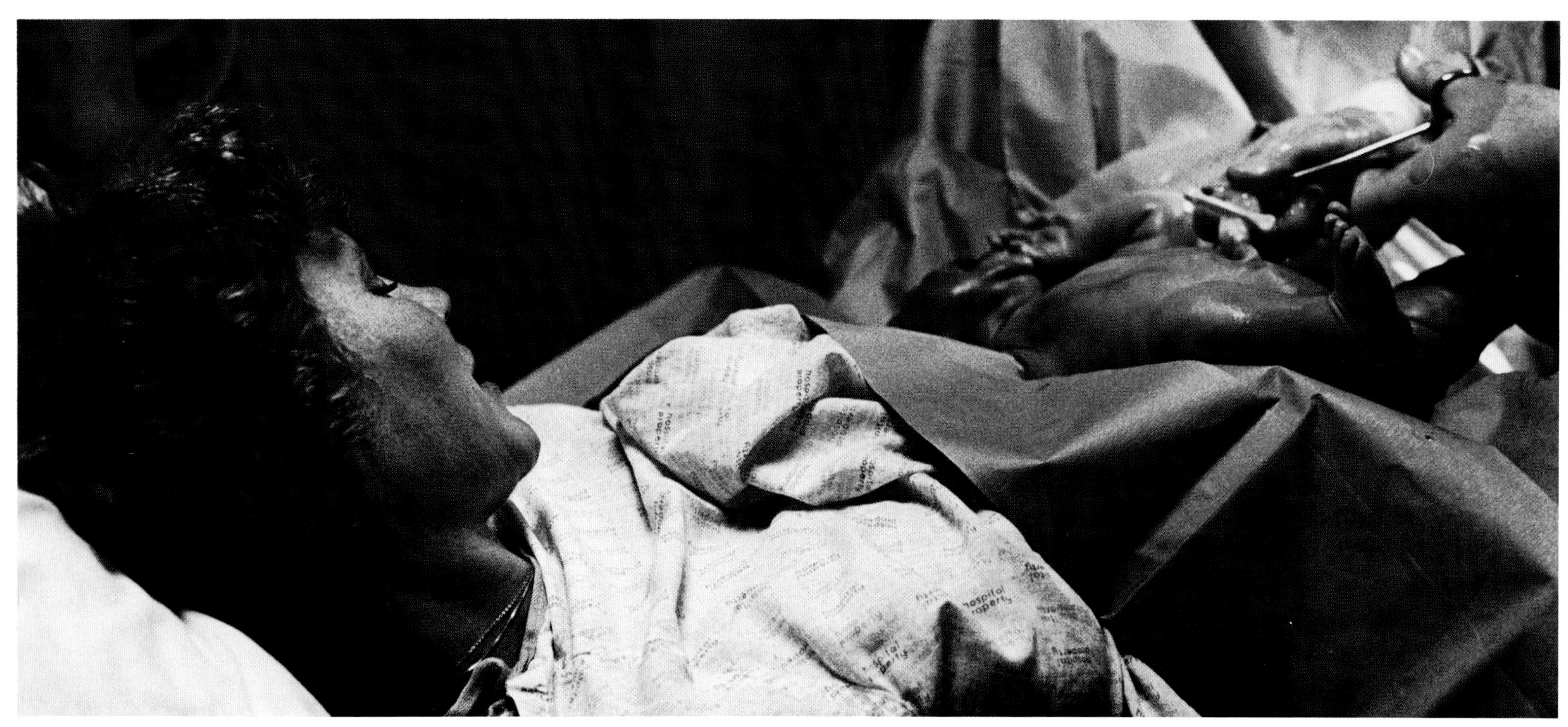

I was in love with everybody
when I walked out of the room,
my face was glowing

and you weren't even the one
having the baby.
your eyes electric
you chanted
the woman
like some tribal chief
led with sounds a-aaah, aaa-aaaah,
the doctor   the husband   the nurse
listened, moved to her moves,

many hands
timed right
like pulling a kite to wind
aaaaaaaaaaah
aaaaaa-aaaaaah,
caught the baby
and birth light

everyone
listened to the mother
as if the whole world stopped

all the way home
you cried
I was robbed

Underground

Nine o'clock somewhere near
Victoria Station. No moon.
The clatter, the call of wheels
of a London subway
pulls me
two at a time
down black steps
to the underground.
It is time to go home.

People are standing
against tile walls,
sitting on benches.
Many of us settlers from the colonies.
Women in veils, women
with stars painted on their foreheads.
Women, men, in suits.
Men whose hands know
the laying of stone,
the cutting of trees.
Beside me, a woman
in a sari the color of leaves
nurses her baby.
The child is wrapped in soft wool
and a language
that fits awkwardly in my ears and
naturally
within my blouse.

I remember lips of sweet sucking
that my babies left there years ago.
Within the silence of strangers,
there is talking.

Eyes of women who work in offices,
eyes of women who live under veils,
all watch the child, the mother,
each other.
The sound of sucking moves
from woman to woman
like the pen of a cartographer.
It is time to go home.

Mother country,
we go back lifetimes to find you
blinking at the light of us
running over this heavy belly of time.

Corser / Adler 49

 Corser / Adler

Mother Tongue

for Allison

Child, you untwisted this struggle
to speak. I lay
on my back at the beach,
hands pressed to my belly.
Water lapped my legs
with shells and leaping fish.
I felt you move
inside me
for the first time.
Your legs, your arms
braille
stuttering across my palm.
I lay against the warmed back of sand
as you lay against mine.
Water surrounded me too.
It seemed like the hum of the ocean
stopped
and I slipped into another time.
As a small child, I was drawn
day after day to the dining room,
to its circle of mirrors, one on each wall.
I would pull over a stool, climb up,
see myself repeated infinitely.
I would touch the glass
wherever it held my faces.

At the ocean, my blood lit
with you inside me,
I was able to see
what I had only sensed:
that the I that I am
is a we.
In my infinite mirror
I am a caravan of people
traveling sand together
through time.
I am the sweat
of a stranger's child in fever,
the sleepless eyes of a friend
packing her son's bag for war,
the ancient chant of a rabbi
uncovering the mirrors of the dead.
Their pain mixes like blood.
Child, I have been a foreigner
on this shore.
I have lost my mother tongue.
Yet sometimes
it comes floating back briefly
not in words
but in moments like this
bodies within body
unslipping the knots of silence.